Several Dances

Also by Maurice Scully

Books
Love Poems & Others
5 Freedoms of Movement
The Basic Colours
Priority
Steps
Livelihood
Sonata
Tig
Doing the Same in English
Humming
A Tour of the Lattice

Booklets
Prior
Certain Pages
Over & Through
Prelude, Interlude & Postlude
Tree with Eggs
Work

Art Object
Numbers [with Coracle Press]

e-chapbooks
Five Dances
Rain [signed piece]

CD
Mouthpuller

Children's
What is the Cat Looking At?

Maurice Scully

Several Dances

Shearsman Books

First published in the United Kingdom in 2014 by
Shearsman Books
50 Westons Hill Drive
Emersons Green
BRISTOL
BS16 7DF

Shearsman Books Ltd Registered Office
30–31 St. James Place, Mangotsfield, Bristol BS16 9JB
(this address not for correspondence)

www.shearsman.com

ISBN 978-1-84861-336-2

Copyright © Maurice Scully, 2014.
The right of Maurice Scully to be identified as the author
of this work has been asserted by him in accordance with the
Copyrights, Designs and Patents Act of 1988.
All rights reserved.

ACKNOWLEDGEMENTS
Ahadada books [web], *Burning Bush* 2 [web], Dedalus Press,
eKleksographia [web], *Gathered Here Today, Golden Handcuffs Review,
Great Works* [web], *MATERIALPoetry*, Oystercatcher Press,
Past Simple [web], *Smithereens* [web], *Succour,
The 15 Project* [web], *Veer Off, Wurmfest*.

Grateful thanks to all concerned.

Contents

On a Light Ground: Eye Dance	13
On a Dark Ground: Work Dance	15
Lyric: Bal/ancing	18
Mountain Railway: Gavotte	20
Miniature	21
Tango	22
Sunlight	23
Just to Say (for tom-tom)	24
Imprint Studio	26
For Treated Piano	29
Tap Dance	30
Thorns Spindles Twigs	34
Sonnet: Print	38
Baint an Fhéir	40
Bluebells in a Wood: Waltz	41
Exposure: Tuesday	44
Klee-like (for glockenspiel)	45
Ballad	46
Ground	47
Walk Dance: The Artist & His Model	49
Heart	51
Blackbird: Jig	53
Geometric (for gamelan)	55
Rain [signed piece]	61
A Stupendous Idea	68
Parallax: on Vellum	69
Song: Dance [knots in the grain]	71
Sonnet: On Tiptoe	74
Butoh: Coup de Soleil	75
Ballad [Irish]	80
Winter	81
Descending a Staircase	82
[Hungarian] Folk Dance: Artist's Studio	84
To Balance	87
Studio Stamp	88

Thread-Bridge (for clarinet)	89
Jig: Blizzard	92
This to Say: Sonnet (drums)	93
Rain Dance	95
Setting (for guitar)	98
Carpet of Memory	100
Locket	101
Uic aithan	102
Poetry	103
Mazurka	104
Pavane	108
Song Beginning 'When'	110
Echo	111

CODA

Village & Interior (with glockenspiel)	115
Jig	117
Orbit	120

Notes	125

Backing Vocals	129

Several Dances
[for voice]

for Bob & Daisy

Sunlight is
on things.

                Frank Samperi

On a Light Ground: Eye Dance

Dapple of mother-spider
at the centre of its wet
web between a hedge & a
trellis. After work, the

wait. Place your foot
there. Then place it
there. Pitch a rock
in the pond: hear that

difference over there.
I-me-myself are moving
forward
          forward

to that left behind, through
air, to that placed shimmer
ahead. Forward. Carry your
spinning circle, a drop

lands, little by/connects
[pendent speck] reverberant.
Hold still. I do. Move. Stare.
Are you ready? What? To cross

which pattern a/pattern a/
[black] ripple of leaf-shadow
over those books there
restless surges & retreats

smooth fluid undulations
that move across a vase
sketched in to burn care-
fully across representations

of small flowers on a curved
ceramic edge complications.
Pause. Meshes of energies
made visible. A calm [autumn]

morning in which pollen or
a calm autumn morning on
which a drift of rich [yellow]
pollen, a calm autumn morning

'outside [the community of] our
perceptions' in which outside
… which … I think (dab)

a fossil horizon, a dust horizon,
a mud horizon, the recent rising
of a nearby river, another fossil
horizon, one on top of the other

(small paint-marks on my palm,
wonder-swirl skin pattern, red
giant, white dwarf)—yes I

think I'll live here for a bit
not across no but along. One.
      Border. Forever.

On a Dark Ground: Work Dance

past a postage stamp stuck
sideways to the side of a
bookshelf going nowhere in
particular just now

past memory-flashes in tight dark
tangles open to the least access
of light stopped formally in code
in ink on paper in rows [blank]

wrapped up in stillness & expect-
ation &/past a weather here then
another there passing beyond past-
future (coil'd)((2, 3))(together)

weathers hitting the roof with a
red herring once in a blue moon
white as a sheet in a black mood
on a red letter day & so on a

jumble then two more (one ornate—
one spartan) take note coming all

the way down to treetops laughingly
referred to *as*. past that through
several nests one in particular I
remember *oh* down along an

uptilting branch through the
bark the feathers the downy warm
woven against the storm past
that sun catching green cloth

through glass here we go thorns
spindles twigs new & auton-
omous additions to the world
not representations of it

cackled an elderly stretcher
behind a canvas all dried up
scrap that sip yr tea Cranach
the Younger Scully the Unsub-

missive a tiny scalded insect
from a desk-lampshade for instance
to the page-top until *he was well-
loved* yr very breath disappears it

holding the falling world *he was
well-loved as an artist and as a
man* holding the falling world well.
who is that figure turning into

the doorway to go? a skull re-
members embers to re-invigorate
me-me-me-me-me/so. I'll deal you
plastic squares of the Absurd while

you shuffle the Possibilities-of-
the-Ridiculous over there, okay?

            done.

intent at desk in shed. relaxed
at table. reading in bed. working.
dreaming. breathing. drinking tea.
spearing fish spelling it out won-

dering wandering pondering
weaving a willow basket or two
on the damp riverbank billows of
mist over water at dawn. rules:

the ludicrous. the fragile. the
        indefensible.

give me some money. give me some
money to live. I'm willing to work.
I'm willing to work well. I'm willing
to work well and apply what talents

I have to the job. you will not get all
of me no but then I'll not get all of yr
money. give me some money. give
      me some money now.

Lyric: Bal/ancing

It's resolved.
This is what you need:
the wheels on the road
go *then—then—then*.

I draw the line
you do too
it's a blackbird
on a rooftip addressing

the neighbourhood
where all's in place
moving apart
& disappear–
ing leaving a trace.

How's yr hearing?
Pressed to the paper
ink wet softest at
the apical bud

                        rend-

                              ered into

alpha-

      bet out of

   the mouth

            &

         memory

                     seed-

                            pod

       burst & …

   & stones settle into
   their foundations
   in silence again.

   Watch them settle
   (no talking please)
   down here well.

Mountain Railway: Gavotte

Drop a pebble in a pool: listen to it. Its
blue glistens. Black-gold-black. To glint,
tremble, stop. I turn off the radiator,
turn on the desk-lamp, sit, start. Here we
are. Soft pulses of light threading a small
hollow to contain the main phase in a fibrous
nest & the next move, the next move, one true
shimmering altercation. Then see. Oh all claim
that. Then don't. Let liars work, enough is
enough as they say (vexed proof), into their
    own dark trap. Drop a pebble in a pool,
            bow.

    You plug the kettle in, hear it boil, is
    that the phone? Cup, spoon, milk. Good.
    Do you really know then what you're about?
    Say: work-shadow by screen-glow, here is
    the chorus that throws us more than (Who?)
    we can ever predict, crest on crest each
    ripple moving out carries light into its
    next receptive fold. Two crows fly low
    following their shape exactly in the clear
    sheen of the wet sand spread flat [tilt sur-
    face to reduce glaze] underneath upside-
    (beat for beat)-down. To land. Hello? Yes?
    By the wave's edge. Holding a lit match, its
    wavering apex, glint of sap below the heat-
    line—each decisive moment, each precise
         flick—drop it in the dish & go.
            Now.

Miniature

Listen: sip coffee from a china cup

still alive

look

good

    [glass

good

luck

hot till olives

drop off that tiny tree up

there

till then. Still. Good.

Listen.

Tango

To know every branch of those trees
beside that house & to climb each one
as a little boy & linger up there, head in the sky
       2, 3, 4 swaying
            so that
in the year of Possibility, first Month of Release,
fourth day of Abjection, if we step here, then there,
then return & repeat that, tap block, here, look, step,
too, there, feeling, wheeling along—what then?
Thumb, middle finger, the little & ring acting as light
supports to the wrist moving in its bony balance holding
the stem & point inking across to thought & eye in a world
placed bright way through.
        Then what? One.
  One year later into one year later into step by step
it would seem the paper to the pen laughing, sip tea,
said, think, feel the tension in the wires relax—
your notebook on a pile of books open at eye-level
slant-wise changing your writing to meet it nib-level to
paper. Blunted blades, powdered shrapnel.
   Then step down the corridor—underpaid
cleaning staff spirited away—with a click of your
steel-tipped cane & a dance, through time, why not—
one-two, one-three-two-one—& (at the Moment of Impact
   & Passing Evidence) turn the lights off
      on your way out. Okay?
      Then.

Sunlight

Then you can put this small stone against that one there on the table
with a click & stand back, to think. It's in the circle of the mind
as much as an aural shiver between two things present.
A stone so light it puckers not at all the cloth underneath.
Beside another so small it is a pool, of waiting.
How a single shiver on the surface changes everything.
How sunlight on a mountain village re-divides solidity.
I folded a piece of paper & let it fall into the bin.
What's that all about? Whose life is this? Where's the dog?
The money? Everything.
The wolf in the plot has a forest made for it,
then it fits, a glove, a cloak, fur, politics.
Curved lines of light dissolving into leaf-tip over leaf-tip.
Terms, conditions, fog at the mouth of the tunnel.
'S an t-airgead?
In the child's language—long ago & far away—'dance'.
Then that stone, put that stone in yr hand beside this one
here on the table, its sound ready, its space already occupied,
for this boy, here, preoccupied, small, to stand back,
to think. Stand back, melt. Stand back, invent. Back-to-back. Meant. Stand.
I dteanga an ghasúir—rince.
In the child's folding land-ridge—long ago & far away—echoes
echo everywhere. Everywhere. So.
Solid. Blend. Sink. Breathe. Chance.

Just to Say
[for tom-tom]

I have eaten
the plums
that were in
the icebox

I have taken
the peaches
that were in
the fridge

  so cold
  so sweet

& the cereal
(*that* was nice)
with its chopped
vivid

strawberry bits
sunflower pips
too—chewy—yes—
I came back I

did I came back
twice for those &
yr eyes feisty & a
little yoghurt.

I have eaten
the plums
that were in
the icebox

& a slice of
rippled colour
where threads
snap & a gull's

wings shiver
slightly in the breeze …
Mice? In *my* kitchen?
No way, José!

To enjoy a bit of
obvious parody-pop now
& again without even
once mentioning the

lice poem dream
thingy
       I have
       I might
       I will
is not a bad thing
in itself (stamp) slim
fingers silvery nails
their black eyelashes

quietly beating one
evening in France in
the what 19th century
    [I have eaten
     the plum's dark
     twisting & spin-
     ning round the
     sparkling stack]
or life's odd angles

splitting its sides—
sexual entanglements
politics envy—just like
to say without losing

the head this side
the flowerbed it was
all very
        really
delicious—& tingly.

    Thanks.

Imprint Studio

Five four zero eight three two zero one
the very early morning sun, the quiet,
the breeze, its sounds in the leaves
outside, clack of magpie, whisper of
the pen on the page. Listen, take it down,
how many dark patches, how much stippled
handwriting, how many little impact
bits there now? Pluck a dandelion: its
stem pops—oozes: one white o.

But what's the bloody use if you can't
make peace, go out, meet people, eat, drink,
laugh—*gabble-gabble-gabble*—as it
grows around its pergola, gossip-blossoms
vicious-petalled, strange-scented?
High speed collisions of tiny ideas in yr
customized bubble chamber under the table.
Tough bright balls of pressed pellets of
poison too

        woven
      through
        a water-
      spout
        from a
      stone
        fish's
      mouth
        here
      where
        light
      hits the
        back
      of the
        fountain
      behind
        a fig &

       bramble
           covered
       lane
           to the
       gardens
           below the
       village
           near the
       mountains
           & the
       strong reg-
           ular song
       of water
           hitting
       water in
           the bottom
       of a trough
           just

       laughs

       laughs

       laughs.

Droplets of connective gel you
take in as a child, personal ornamentation,
quietly unique idiosyncrasies—minúte,
unrecorded, disappearing—keep their
place in their fluidly mapped geometry,
an abstract system made tangible through
language's spiralling ribboning as you
lived it until they disappear altogether
with you forever under a stone somewhere.

It may be in the detail, I don't know,
that slight ache, moments fitting moments
that undulate & fade & leave a faint
fabric on yr wrist they may call memory

on this planet. Hard to say. They say *whisper-whisper-whisper & history's history & flowers push flowers into being & what time is it, over there &…* ? Yes, I think I say, I don't know.

For Treated Piano

POEM

Here I am they write.
Dot. What's it to you? Dot.
Saturday December 1st. Dot.
The best is potentially the worst.

OTHER POEM

They take a poem of yours
& put it in a book called *Other*.

They always knew this, Father & Mother,
a bit of a genius, sure,
but what'll become of him?

That future is here now
& it's no *poem*.

HERE: NOW

You still can't keep still in its jar.
Can you? Label it & sell it we
suggest. You suggest a price. Nice.
A crease in the storm. Warm?
What? Who thought out this
bit of prize-carp coming tumbling
through that chute to us here now—
Hi There!—splat. Culture troubles
weigh me down. People are tiny.
    Get over it you clown.

Tap Dance

Artists
in their
factories
are

working
hard now
filling in
steel

boxloads
of grant
application
forms

on an
ongoing
shift
basis

through the
generations
beyond
making.

Life is
good.

There is
breathing
space.
The

galleries
are show
ing the
normal.

Formal.
The avant
garde. The
pig in a

  poke.

Elderly ladies
eyes closed
heads lifted
listen to

  mell
  if
  luous

poetry
& no
body's
bitter.

  .

Dips from
its pergola
touching yr
head as you

pass a rose by
way of caress
on a chill bright
winter morning

turning on its
stem pale
cream along a
black path

into the
park

sometimes
the slits
of an owl's
lids open

to watch a
drop

falling from a
horn of lime
hanging from the

underarch
of a bridge.

.

O
come dance
with me
ye

prety maidens
& hark the foulys
song along an
avenue

of Boojum where
huge pyramids of
crystal new-fangled
interwoven

logics laugh at
the little people
tiny down there
among the

latest splashes
of the
hyper-baroque.

It's good
to be
dead.

Past the
pastoral fascists
& gallery
thugs.

Pluck that
string. It
really feels
like this…

cycles
within
cycles.

And a dog
out there in
the dark going
Art! Art-Art!

Art!

Thorns Spindles Twigs

here we
see a monk
       dip
          dab
              tip
                    delineate

in a mountain-
top temple

    twisting
        ripples
            spills
                down in-
to an eroded rockpool—

    black—

    on the
    water-paper
    surface—

    writing—

    piping
    distinct
    ly through

    clear air now
    echoing now

    disappearing
    into a breeze

    now back
    in a different key—

here you are
in a shed in a garden
in the cold wondering what's
the next
move

(in a trap)

here he is reviewing his life
chuckling/snarling
letting the pen drop—*cheese!*—

    magpie on tree-tip:

                  bal.
                      an.
                            cing.
  …

talk to me
in the clear   passing/
real things   again
now
    push the

ferry out   push
sorting & storing
pebbles
        road tar
blue after rain

blue sheen of
the dew of heaven
skeleton of light
in a

leaf
    twisting
on

      a
          stem
touched

moves/d again
slight gash top
left-hand/otherwise
near
    fine.

lay the space bare where you can.

   …

the cypress the yew &
the pine all
move

differently in the same
wind. locked
into

the anthill, the Normal Routine,
carrying yr fleck
in a

tunnel you wake, dreaming. a long
time. after-
wards

outside (always afterwards, The Outside)
a still dawn
a still

quiet dawn; stillness, ever-remembered
fore-forewarned
star of

mica/gull turning; did that
small wave
catch

a moment then breathe back into
its sister move
then?

& then/in the grammar. braille-
touched, the side of.
tangled.

if that's a calculation this is a
stone wearing the air
away.

draw back…

    this then suddenly

    untouch, touch, wings,
    map-map, count then
    hibernate then track

        blizzard
        immense
         this
         then
        possible

the becomes inconceivable the when
  mind the in acceleration terrific a

        .

      put cup down
        it rings
     when I lift it
     up down again
       a song.

        .

Sonnet: Print

Pale moon-print on roof under black sky, long, thin,
song of a single siren in the distance, a snail-shell,
a car goes by, a silver tongs in a bowl
                I was extending my
                left hand to drop a
                crumpled paper
                ball into a bin
Discomfort in twisting round discomfort in
mind in time when birdsong is heard fluidly
arriving from under a tree outside
                Drop it into a bin.
                I'd decided on something
                else & had crumpled up
                that sheet & dropped it in
                the bin. Decided to Oh
Another approach to the origin of the
solar system is a comparison of solar &
planetary compositions
                A wire-mesh thing on the floor.
                Can't remember where it came from.
                Norway? Sweden? Tossed my piece
                of paper casually over a shoulder &
                landed it landed with a little papery
                tick into its… target.

Planetary & solar compositions must have been
almost identical at the outset. Or is that true
to say? At some stage a small amount of its gaseous
mass must have been left behind by the contracting
proto-star
                Tock! went the ball of
                paper in the bin. I pressed it
                together, took aim, & tapped
                it into the bin. A satisfying
                bull's eye. But to continue.
                I put it in the bin. Now.

Now I'll write a poem. Now I'll write a piece
of music. Now I'll put the poem to the music
cutting & trimming & adding happily in these
twilight years in the dark. *Clang! Bang! Whang!*
Hey!
     Put *that* in a bin.
     Lever it into a bin.
     Deftly—into the bin
     with it.
I carry too much about with me anyway, you do too.
Who can do less? All this past. And ridiculous
futures projected, layer over layer…
     Pitch them into their bin.
     Get a new bin if necessary.
     Drop them in. Listen for that
     small *thock* as they reach
     bottom: *hah!*
Words are so useful & pleasant. Don't you think?
Biro, sandwich, tarmacadam. Yes, madam? Meanwhile
on the moon… Put that in, take it out, sit down
again to write it down again.
     And put it in a bin. Put it—
     gaps tapped together make
     a sharp arc in air—bowl it
     over into the/when one & one
     is one-one what can a toucan
     do?/ta-ra/bin/ink-splash/there.

Baint an Fhéir

Poem: Plod. *Poem*: What's left of your bones.
There, see. *Poem*: 'Blunder follows blunder'
he wrote, (tapping the floor) beginning again to
take note, and grow up. Little incidents connect
to make a fabric where air meets in its heat cold
too to the lip tangible in its flow, woven through,
walled in. The verb: *gathering*. The verb: *locate*.
The verb: *stop*. Acumen, praise. White is the colour
of your true love's hair—Wood Angelica, Butterbur,
Purple Loosestrife—now. Yes. The verb: *to see*.
        The verb: *to know*. This then.
                So.

Bluebells in a Wood: Waltz

The larger the chimneys the higher
the family's status in the town—
little humanity reaching up…

Step by step as you go
pressing grass down in patches in yr path,
predictable in direction but not discrete location,
making small boot-pools of a deeper green
in dew   here, here…

& then we…

Mist rising from the river in a wide fold
stops. Making noise inside one's self
beside one's self & fluidly making
things up as you go

moisture rising in tiny threads

from one side the plate-glass window
night street people float by—
tourists, goodly citizens
turning home—flash! flash!—thread by thread—
while on this
side
we

had the most

a flower-shoot shifts a crumb that, disturbed,
falls back

the most wonderful…

& a green blade points to light—
at yr age look to yr home—the earth—the world—

& then we

but seriously—
                        switch the light on, flick the match
to spirt & burn the ready wick—
                                  an apple falls

to have the… the most wonderful

you're born, you breathe, you learn, learn not to, to
choose one way, then another, feeling to steer along in the dark, sometimes,
sometimes roughly swept from room to room, rock to rock, while

all the time having the most

you know there's nothing
there's absolutely nothing quite like a hot mug of tea
in the door of a cold shed in a garden on a late October morning
steam mixed with mist
warming the hand, the heart, the face,
the work, & waking

to have the

birds signal & bicker   leaves stay still

wonderful

fruit trees stopped in winter

most

grassblades bend under last night's rain

full   *having the*

tilting

& getting yr mind too
too far into the piece on hand
it may be   then to pull back

to note a plant-stem curve & a flower follow
round to light—three, four—through glass

watch it & know turning the dance touch hands

elbows lightly I—
threading & stitching—

wonder if

that soft down on forearm
little tickle of the soft down
of yr forearm

if

the most

flash   step by step as you go

the most wonderful… having the most wonderful

in time

wonderful time.

Exposure: Tuesday

Cleaning my glasses with a cloth
she made for me as a child years ago
round & round with care & pleasure
each small lens tilted, glinting—distant
blue mountains, dust devils over the plain,
child-shepherds descending from the hills
to circle & look at you, yr van broken down
in the middle of nowhere in Lesotho—so that I
could read &—lost in the fume & dark of the
foundry—click of the plant as you pull &
it snaps, white dot of sap at the stem-head,
a grey woodlouse disappearing under clay—
touch hands lightly, bow down, one step,
two—years ago this child stitching this piece
of cloth for me needle to soft cotton patiently
at her table so that I could clean my glasses
round well here now to read & maybe one
day dammit look the world square in the face
                & see.

Klee-Like
[for glockenspiel]

It is 6.40 am.
It is Boxing Day.
It is St Stephen's Day.
It is Wednesday,
Woden's Day.
It is early morning December
in a garden in Dublin, dark.
It is a point [A] in a life-space.
It is, if it is ever read by another,
a record of point [A] drawn to
that point in 'yr' reading 'this'
[oil & watercolour & pen on burlap on board]
a floating ['mysterious'] point [B]. *Tock.*
It is 6.47 am. It is dark,
silent, cold. From point [A]
in the Landscape of the Suppressed Mystery
to you in the Citadel of [B],
a glinting silver triangle
on a dark green ground. Don't move. Or
do. Point [C]. It is not to be believed, the oddity of
True Stories, The Wolf in the Fairytale,
The Girl in the Wood, stopped &
waiting, in potentia. The letter E,
the word OH.

Ballad

Moon drips blood pooling under a black tree,
fingers, eyelashes, voices, distance—wait, do
you know this tune?—Saturday night, hag with
gold sovereigns, boy with red hair, girl with
a shock of blaze, that silver egg that/Hit is
ful mery in feyre forest to here the foulys song/
She moved closer to her & thought how odd
to look like other people on the street & yet—
drabs, pickthanks, bribe-takers—this feeling of
detachment was so strong/makin a mane/A
branch moves, wings slide sideways in silhouette,
ripples spread to a dark rock. Stop. In ahint yon
auld fail dyke/that spiritual creative energy that
permeates all life (yes) & stimulates growth.
Bird-eye, grass-wisp. *Isn't it delightful when
there's been a soft fall of snow?* I lov'd her well,
good reason why/ 'Symbolic of mankind's never-
ending striving for perfection, flying as a motif
occurs again & again.'/had he but a mouth of
gold to kiss/where be ye my mery maidens?/
arthropods, sponges, priapulids, annelids, medusoides,
algae &/His lady's tain anither mate/*Years might
pass, she told herself, but the day would come
when*/into my green green garden oh/*would come
when he would remember her*/here is the, here is
the 9 o'clock knightly, inhale, exhale, a tradition's
a tradition & repetition's repetition, here is the, here
is the, (I see what my father saw in the sea now) red,
black, silver, shiver, water, red, black, here is the, here
is the news. Fol-de-dee-di-do. Rigid grid. Good.
                    Grid. Bad. Grid. Good.

Ground

Then pieces break off the first and hit
upper layers of a subsequent that tilt into
a previous half-established abandoned.

Then another fell to that (even in wrong
handwriting) and on its side and fed into
little balancing pans unevenly, stitching its
oddities together. Here we go. *C'era una volta…*

Broken decisions   crumbled decisions   flashes
of jagged fractures   inner honeycombs of old
bones   yellow   in the Cloud Museum of the Later
Upper Ego Period   life   each side the glass
stopped   then sliding past   crushed rage-paper
crimpled exits   a magpie in the cherry   a cat
on a conifer stump   tiny shadows on birch-bark
I… I… I…

Hexagonal combs of decisions filled with sweet
and sticky pulp. Step. When X rolls over O.

Orchidaceous decision-shimmers   Delicate Ache
  Delicate Regret   Delicate Descent   Millions
of little plant-cups brim with liquid sugar.

My wad of apothegms is bigger than your wad of
apothegms. X. P. K.

Rounding a corner early one fine May morning
44 years ago in short trousers as the custom then
was (so different from the skirts, robes, taffeta-
lined embroidered bodices and plastic tabards of
today) tin whistle piping *Oh For Marie's Wedding*—
or some such nonsense—the boy knocked against
another boarder (this was at the ELIGP) so that
the whistle's mouth-piece jabbed sharply into his
upper palate. So La Ti Do. Thus marked out for

language at an early age, at precisely the *right* age
in fact: 10 years, 3 months, 3 days. Words and Music.
Or perhaps it was *Do Bhíos Lá i bPortláirge*.

Deciding always to have your private-mind
in… in fact losing the skill to impart your
full-mind. One, true; two, howbeit. Goe litel
boke, reade the rocks. Go prety fascicle—flee,
floor, dive, bricks—swim.

Walk Dance: The Artist & His Model

Stepping to work under trees in fog one morning early,
droplets collecting on branch-tips, surfaces dissolved
then glistening into focus, threading the siphon where
pets check territory & grid, my late father appeared,
walking, late …

        cover over reveal & recover

keep in the mind, in its place place, mind, spacious,
otherwant elsetouch. One link impresses echo on another.
Tap. You wake up. Bullied into sleep

        cover over reveal &

years of grief years years of grief years of   the
fruit's skin lives, its grooved lines shiver & expand

        cover over

past a quietness, that space luminous where a tree had
been/to/on the way to my/on the *glé*/on the/to a/to gather
about oneself a power/life tightened, ice thinning & seems
to splinter into what is called the past, placing scraps of
recorded footsteps down here, down there, the future
(modified), the present simple, the present perfect, the
present fragments …

        this

threads everywhere

        story (   ) this story

a bowl, a pinecone, a tree,
leaf-shadow shifting to the side
of yr left eye as you follow the page
& read *partitions* for *apparitions*

soft thud of a large timber hitting earth—
this, a light hum in yr ear
a tiny
beetle round the edge of the
bright
new
page
    moving...

Now I am listening. Now I am hearing. Now I am talking to you.

Heart

You watch a dream pause
over a pool in a forest
under a breeze rippling its
surface reflections of inverted
branches & a patch of sky where
one bird flies by, upside-down.
Let it slow down.
Down.

A train is moving along.
What stations are we coming to
now? It feels like a late station.
Clack of wheels on steel on
wooden trestles that creak as
the carriages go by slow through
rocky overhangs somewhere
on the outskirts of a shadowy

small town. Down. Out past
Self-Dramatization. Moving across
teeming alleyways, uncinate appendages,
the wavering varieties & all their little
dots out there where a clock stops at
twenty past two. Twenty past.
For an intervening year or two.

Where a herd of sheep & goats—
bells clonking, pebbling the village street,
snapping at greenery—pass by into the shadows.
Gone. Wing-flap. Birdsong, tree-song, floated, tilted,
moving away on its own scrap of independent energy
where everything lives, however briefly,
beating its one small heart. The person
at 4310 does not subscribe to this service.

This session cannot be continued
at this time. Barking little chants

of love. How did you ever end up
making so many calls to call them
in yr twilight years-years (Please
try again later). And gimme the
voice-mail blues.
Years.

All the covers
of these books
were designed
by some guy
called *Raw*.

Why?

Blackbird: Jig

Stop now & listen round the bough-top
I mean hang on a bit at the bus stop is that
Patric & his pals giving us the nod or is it
hi there yeah looking myserious, what's up?
   Pop yr laptop in yr satchel, he said,
      let's go.

We'll give pleasant lectures at expensive
universities paddling happily along not
rocking any coracle or canoe between
overhanging willows of Fiction & Non
he said, a quiet by-water by a prize-rich
     sluice. How about you?

Mellow me with alcohol on a chilly winter's
night followed by a little loving—who could
say no to that, right?—while dabbling in this
pool between fiction & its opposite: what do
    you think? You might?

Cards slap tables through the day hey-ho—
Polyurethane, Dust-Bin, Dart-&-Grab.
What's it all about? Is it Friday? I don't know,
I need money. Scratch your head, kill the itch,
that histrionic heart (with the hand on it) or that
other on that dark stairwell fading up from … what?
Gaps in the game? Stark bright bugle of a daffodil.

  Slip, tug, thread. Where am I now?
   And are you with me?
    Hey

nonny nonny. This is a day. This is a
moment in a day. Shadow-leaves move
more lightly behind your head (than in it)
in yr hut-in-hiding & seem to shiver
through the delicate outlines of their life

    & after-mark. Take care. Has this ever
        happened to anyone before?
        Who can tell. What the hell.
            Ring a bell?

Geometric
[for gamelan]

I hadn't realized that
that bird-phrase from
that magpie is quite
that of a laying hen's
too till now as languages
overlap & slap together
making a music you're
making a music you're
too busy trying to catch
to really notice that house
you passed last night by
chance for instance you
part grew up in where cars
pass, pass. Odd & solid.

.

    There's the past.
    Here's the future.
    A to B, connect.
    Watch this ball.
    A to B to B
    to A. Slap, tear.
    When a dandelion's
    picked it pops: its
    white sap, its
    stark ring, its
    little laugh. There
    is so much bird-
    song in this pocket
    of presence too we
    recommend you stop
    now & listen to
    the bough-top. Good.

           To the Blackbird of
           Triangulation, Cats
           & Scribal Memory.
           Before moving on.

                  . .

             Where the page
              curves in to its
              binding & light
             pours down from
             an overhead lamp
             like that (like this)
              eyes meet surface
              stitch with stitch
              text to one side
             image to the other
                 & laugh.
                  Sparks.
                   Print.
              And start again.

                  . . .

From this beach here you can watch a cargo ship
come in to port, a jet tilt turning to land, a sky
lark rising in its translucent tube of what could
be its flight to vantage & descent along that rippled
territorial abstract that descends gently here to you

                lost among
                steel plates
           ropes pulleys winches
              welding cradles
                at a bench
              in a workshop
              in the shadows
             at the back of the
           Black Glowering Factory
            I mean Foundry of the

well
the…
Imagination.
Toodle-oo.

Wind sand waves
hiss as they
make contact
with what
someone
at some stage
somehow got to call
reality
(I think)
& break & start
to slide past
that last mark
yr feet made
on the ground
again.
A quarter past
two.
What's it to you?
Falling together
(fissure, monument)
and gathered
in one.
Before moving on.
Good.

. . . .

writing a little poem for
someone directly in
that way something
I almost never do
but in this dream
working content
into the shade out of
the heat with a light

stick in the sand until
a detail in the distance

fats & thins where a bird
on a far wall clears
(the impossible poetry
of the closed heart chakra)
comes, goes, watching
that slight movement
in the shade in the morning
in hunger (flower-edges
flare back) so much so
much in whiteness gone

it was rough notes
smooth ideas & a
willowy chorus
brought us thus far
dear writing something
for someone directly in
the shade under the
moving trees there
in an outburst of
description & the absurd
over a flat watercolour
on some plaster priming
on gauze mounted
on cardboard.

. . . . .

Is that enough? A little-dog bark, two tones, incessant, with regular 5/10 intervals: *off-off. Off-off. Off-off.*

.

Clubbed antennae, coiled proboscis—*that's him!*

.

A memo is not an omen.

.

I always thought. Until we got stuck in the airport.

.

'255 Material' is written on a box on a top shelf.
'SuperValu—*values you!*' is printed on a box
beside it. Not content with nocturnal flights of
the imagination in yr tent I can't really see what
you meant. Well.

.

An omen fits its moment. Neatly. At least.

.

So dark the morning it could be almost night.
That time of year here when it's hard to tell.
But tell me.

.

Memorable omissions, no mention of aim,
mean tones, amen. Label that.

.

Your eyes meet the world in the morning: a box on a
shelf, some books, birds, day-sound of light rain
on a roof, trees moving, distant traffic. Beg a
question, get an answer. Goddess of Worry, release
me, Devil of the Arrow of Time—let fly! Parallels,
diagonals, circles & bent squares, where are we?
Devils of Dimension, disimprison me. Flick through

yr experiential Repertoire, see what happens; listen; forget. Get up! I did. You saw. We played. At last. Is that enough?

Rain
[signed piece]

Stop.

A toddler
playing
with
his

tin bucket
& broken
spade

in a small cracked
black & white
photo from
the 50s

popped out of
a book on
yr desk

leaf-shaped fibulae
spears & shields
a stony ingle
a

quiet cell
in the woods
berries birdsong
rootlets

that
trickle

down
through
separating

earth-crumbs
cuckoo-spit
nettle-stalk
conduits

gullies of fire
whose flames
lick &
twist

around blackened
jagged rocks
rear &
flick

as a fly zips by
overhead
then dis
appears

into
the
light

(

)

h'm or is
it ice melting
in a forest
gully I/stop/

this must
be that
beautiful
little quick

feathered
animal
feeding by
the

wave-edge
just
recently
arrived

to here
here this
piece

one
hitting
another
&

spliced
pips
kernels
shells

with that
dark
shimmer

of
alpha
bets

& grammars
come
down

quietly
on to
the leaves
of

the canopy
in the
garden

where
you
stop to

listen to
look
back

touch

fleck
of paper
caught
in a

bent staple
patterns
in
a

book
opened
on a
table

that make
your
take your
name-

shell
twistedly
melted
into it

(

)

moved
glasses-case
to the left
held page

down
flat like
that so
that

who it's
for is
dully
audible

a white
speck

-door-

sliding
over black
in twilight

become a

-door-

swan each

-door-door-

tree a
sheath of

-door-

moving
moisture
each forest
a colony

of
glistening
spirits

in the
transpir–
ation
stream

between
base &
open
sky

    –

      –

        –

stamp
yr
feet

into
that
pool

there
then
dip this

piece
into this
pot

here then
weave & |
ooze
where

let's see—wow—
flatten it—work |
this |

box
until it gets to
cohere left
to right
                         |
itself & fall
apart again |
too. There. |

    Blob. |

A Stupendous Idea

I woke about four o'clock
the next morning
with a stupendous idea.

Parallax: On Vellum

Moving in quick-time its thin
body pulsing & searching
a little fly lands on my open
copybook moving towards
the letter 'e' & a full-stop
then away quickly opening &
closing its shiny slices in silence…
Water moving by the bank
& further out over the weir
black-brown white-cream
a fish breaks sky in it
rings repeating outwards our
words out towards another
over light invisible breeze-parts
slapping the sides of the corridor
its glass listen listen its glass case
sheet steel each minute a shiver
in the grass three drops on a wide
blade run together…
I went to university for ten years
& learnt nothing. Got a degree.
That teaches you that nothing is
something. I place a rock at a
cave mouth. Who knows what
it is, but it may get out. Trust me.
Moving over the water & the
water moving. One cherry petal
on a snail's black back. Scratch
& cross-hatch, dip, dart then flit
through air-streams for take-off.
Is that the sound of your hand
on a page I wonder the very
name whereof may peradventure
drive into every head a sundry
supposition/hey, where's my
pen? Capture-strands, surface
tension, rain pellets on taut silk

reeled in. Just last week I got a new
one, here we are writing with it now
& it's ok. In fact, I like it. It flows along.
That's what a pen is for. Slap.
Yr glowing bristles in the dark,
yr temporary arrangements in the
larger Temporary Arrangement
of interlaced overall design, pits &
peaks, a piglet upside-down blowing
on a chanter in the margin, its
tune mute, moving over moving
water, ripple & twirl, working,
walking, working, walking off.

Song: Dance
[knots in the grain]

    Sun shines on a quiet Friday morning,
    a dog in the distance,
    not much doing—
                 pigeons—
    cars,
    another dog
    tacks back,
    I lift my cup.
          Sip.
    Then.
    Fly-shadows vanishing into the light again.

.

moving through the estate
              where are my
the lorry
       moving
my books   is-is

the lorry   slowly moving
               slowly through the estate
where are they   is
         what?
              books   estate
which   is-is-is

.

    Leaves in the breeze that waver &
    come back to where they were,
    time measurements
                out of time,
    early summer, late May,
    yr fingers, together, like that,
    a tipi, thinking, absurd habit,

   Dollar Budget (M) printed
   on a plastic pen in yr pocket—
   light through a skylight—
   the sky's light. Right. Then.

   .

woven together
       to hear the pages
    to press a feather
        to hear the pages fall
to how many
    together
         to charred in pits
     whispering
  between the rails
      between the towns
 oh they say weigh this & these my books up *oh*

children robbed now of childhood now
adults of care now
compassion packaged & for sale now
poor of power
languages of grip
cores disappear this-this what's new?
      hello? yes? who?

    Taste.

    Let.

    Tell.

& the lorry moving
      through its
        they-they
     shivering blank-blank estate.

 .

Apple & pear petals disperse & float
& drench the air
     while a bird alights in another rhythm
on the pink & white.
Early summer. I lift my tea.
In a corner by the window a little black phone
comes to life. Sip. Hello, satellite! You're break/ink up—
Several Ideas in B Flat, for Oboes & Guitars—
pup link—*in improbable time, moderately wild*—
pops out of the blank-blank is-is blank-blank
is-is-is.

.

Gathered up in their ground-pit & fallen into this
pool, hissing with a splash, deep, dark, sinking,
where wavelets circle upwards, outwards slapping
together, disappearing, each in turn. Burn. A mist &
its structure curls round a house, a branch, a tree-shape,
a streetlamp, a door-lock—following—or a single
bright green leaf that holds a little air-water, then
drops, from its tip—silver, globed, gravity-happy—
  one piece. These are the backing vocals.
   (But for whom?)

    Yes.

   I lift my cup.

A lorry is moving slowly through the estate.
   Where are my books?

Sonnet: On Tiptoe

Touch a wet surface in just
the right place & you might
find the reward to be a shiver
of what you thought was well
a sweet appreciation of the next
breath. *Scrape-scrape-scrape*
go the implements on the path,
this & then this, one syllable
it may seem louder than another,
my fingers, your eyes, a steel
shutter opening in the laneway,
a van door clapped shut. Stop.
That's the thing about frescoes.
Just how fresh for how far into god
they said oopsy-daisy bamboozle
you know the story: here
we are at this point in this blur
in this interglacial, now—tip elbows,
bend the knees, step, look round,
look back, step again, & bow,
what date's today anyway?
Soft-falling snowflakes.
Whispers of sleet on glass.
Even to begin to write letters,
still, little intimacies on folded
sheets in envelopes from
a far countree & stamps licked
& pressed down on the outside
& overprinted with dark marks
of origin, the dew upon her dress
she said, connecting
fetching into the hands of someone
else. Pale. Even that. To come back
from the war. To know no way of being
present again, ever. Listen. Fungal
hyphae & mites' excrements give
leaf-mould its distinctive smell.

Butoh: Coup de Soleil

a small house built by an artist
on two levels hidden among trees
on a hill where birds peck under
a larch & a fly stops on a stone

grooming/nature we call it nature
we say nature & her tripled x-rays
& tiny bones in flight wrapped
round protected enfolded &

difficult to concentrate what's
that a beat then a what slash sound
of/slash/traffic on wet streets
outside. stop. question. cope.

woke on a planet of echo woke
shaken woke amazed woke ready
to re-work all of the preceding
woke on edge woke desperate woke

in visible light hitting a city in
parts a bright bit CV descending
round a core lens deft & around
again at 59 makes sense degrees

  if nothing else does
                older
now go see understanding
  nature's laws the trees

       ( )   ( )

      that

stand on tiptoe as it
were on their claws
tiptoe?

[space illegible]

in what could be

called a descending a
stepped hill a revolving
glass door at its base

shadowy figure must
get past (through) re
volves dangerously but
(wake triumphant)

a series of
meshes of which
yr body is
one (success)
heart pounding

called life
(it could be
called life)

eerie crisp leaflets
in the half-light
nesting/smack on the
cheek/a train past

advertisements for
toothpaste insurance
alcohol flat & wide
4 ways to be right

5 to be wrong—
pods veins curves/
flash/enters the
under-

street here we are
at the base of the
alveolar ridge in debt
sheltering nature

across a deserted
piazza (& ghosts over
what appears there
moving *Hi I'm Miró*

*wing-commander Miró
haven't we met?*) &
the tripled x-rays
& the birds peck

& the semi-visible
float fast into each
other this way &
that laughing

oh ha-a-a-a-appy day!

    to orbit around
the steep liquid spine of
        the
         river
        (so
        & so)
        through
        a
        series
        of
        meshes
        of

which
yr
body
is
one

s
p
i
n
d
l
e

c
r
y
s
t
a
l

i
n

t
h
e

l
i
g
h
t

.

s
u
n

.

a pebble
  on a soapstone
dish beside
  an acorn cup
its thin veins
  between a/open to
a/a split a
  shadowed
in a hollow
  a slit cur[v]ling
back to its
  top side
up
  size of a
small bird's
  egg
cool in yr
  palm.

Ballad
[Irish]

There is a time to growl through the
fence & a time to follow that long shadow
with yr eyes to the beginning of what you
realize is the boot-top of the Giant
tráth drannadh tríd an growl through a
time *'n scáth fada sin a leanúint* with yr
go géar cúramach ó 'sea beginning of
what you *go barr buataise an Fhathaigh*
you
      realize now
there is a time to growl now through the fence
& a time to follow now that long shadow
with your eyes now to the beginning of what
you realize is the boot-top of the Giant.

Winter

glasdubh

'pale black'

signifying

'dark grey.'

Nobody sees

the world as

you do.

Have a nice day.

Descending a Staircase

Ash. Lizard. Rock. Descending through a cloud-layer
to a repeating hall with seating set out in a pat pattern
where audiences resolve in silence against, then into
a blank wall, clap-clap, expectant faces focused—a quiet
arc in the air with yr right hand right there, left hand
following the rail—rose, pillar—cash? visa?

…don't fall—bare mud, nibble at the world—

down the flowing stone stairway to the empty gallery,
carrying yr 'mess of shadows' to the still animate in
two hundred seats in formation each with a pattern of
perforations, an inverted triangle pointing to (space) you.
Breathe in. This must be… what? Detach, transfer.

A silhouette on a staircase slithering past capital
holding the jig-saw up until the cows come home—

& I felt I had had so many things to get done—repeat—
& I felt I had had so many things to get done—repeat—

don't fall, take care, break the tissue, descend,
part cool clouds to see—cold to these fingertips
you've had for so long now, extending, feeling along,
here, and then here, tenuous …

   stoss side scooped
      lee side builds

until a housefly visits & a magpie splashes in the barrel.

Wake up! It's the middle of yr life, you can either
go on blinking, dazzled, on the tarmac, or re-start
yr engines *now*.

   [Laughter]

We are aware, says a breeze, you may not be
wholly there. Tinkle of finches. This must be Art.
At the sharp, dark end of yr pen. *It's not as if …*
she says, *it's not as if you know, you know.* I know,
I say, & mean it, ideas arriving thick & fast under
bubble-wrap in books from the Amazon &—flash!—
everywhere: crowds, trees, lights in mid-afternoon
dark in the rain in the cold—red, green, blue, white—
it must be that Festival of the Death of the Year again …

& everyone's insane. Well, that's a start.

I was going through a few pages of concrete expression
of feeling & imagination the other day—flick, flick—
beautiful, harmonious & illuminating, when the whole
damn shebang dropped out the window & took off into
the blue, water slapping its edges, each wavelet
claiming each echo sweetly for itself (as they do),
Meadow Foxtail, Cat's Tail, Cock's Foot, Rye-grass,
Crested Dog's Tail, False Oat-grass, Yorkshire Fog …

glumes
        paleas
                awns
                        ligules…

[Hungarian] Folk Dance: Artist's Studio

That job application
returned unopened
with a covering letter
thanking you for yr interest
and wishing you every
success in yr future
career Gaudate Deum
close window close it
tight (well) with finality
and panache you know
how it is in the Temple of
Echoes of Work Once Done
and return to the main case…

Symbol-evolving pattern-
obsessed idealistic creature
of cruelty and kindness in the
frustrating chaotic illogical
fantastic meaningless muck of
life you… stop and cede to
close window and return
to main page.

Strike a match, hold it steady,
things ignite the way you say
day goes into night, twist that
and scratch even if things are not
what they seem then close window
to return to main phase.

Look, mark it with yr pen,
the calendar says the 27th
dot dot, a glint, in series,
in eternity, a tiny life—
look up—cold, heat, light—
that tendril following sun

through air rippled around a
stick thinking tra-la beyond thought ...

    seems to read the blurred
    print on the back of the
    packet on the table amid
    the racket.

In reading something about
a 'linguistic event' I spotted
a misprint and went to pencil
it in but pencilled the same
word a line below by mistake
(in which that word was *not*
a misprint)—is that a linguistic
event or just a snippet from
a drifter's ballet? Bullet
snug in its chamber, quiet.

    Is blazoned on the back
    of the packet on the table.
    Stir the soup, tug the cable.

Did Goethe privilege a grand
bourgeois outlook and combine
it with an art which cosmetically
screens out the wrinkles of reality?
I wonder, shaving this morning,
moonlight a delight, but red
a warning.

    Is streaming down the side
    of the packet. A million
    things happen at once. Can
    you hack it? Dogs barking...

Which brings us round again—
ladies step forward as the gents
fall back—to that job application

returned unopened this morning
thanking you for yr interest &
wishing you every success in yr
future career tra-la not so much
that you've just arrived but that
 you'll never get there.

I look, you look, you look, I do.
Dance. A berry drops from a tree.
Here we are. Now. Put that in yr CV.
Engendering a systemic glytch in
the catalyst-catharsis matrix over
the Give/Receive pattern dynamic
so that it is impossible for us at
this moment in time to offer you a
dipped the brush-tip in then let fly
to receptive paper listening-thinking
impossible to offer you a offer you a
 stamp those feet
 & good.

To Balance

      simper
    skit
        wad
    snag

Just the stitches in the fabric—*scuffle, snug, scrub, spatter,*
reef, snip, split, frolic—particularly the stitches in the fabric,
a bridge I know, a little house under it… what is that sound I'm
hearing, a somehow draped structure around a core? The beetle's
upturned body in the sink. My hands waiting for something to happen…

    Do you like it?
    Yes, I do.
    Your shed
    your books
    your notebooks
    your time.

Most populations hardly notice the alphabets they live through,
but when oral cultures come into contact with cultures that write,
'literate' culture—as we say—the oral culture, learning that
alphabet, can move across its symmetries and strangenesses with a
certain… sensitivity. So

    cride é
        daire cnó
  ócán é
      pócán dó

is oral, *and* lettrist—every word rhyming, every syllable
rhyming, every *letter* finding its repetition (except the kiss,
a plosive), a sort of spasm of self-conscious design (Celtic,
bardic, academic even) from far away, in silence, and the Roman
alphabet on goat's skin to the side of a Gospel, in Latin. There.
Just the stitches in the fabric. But a girl's kiss too carrying
across centuries in a handful of received letters. Nine of them
in fact. Now, do the same in English.

Studio Stamp

Squeeze some ink on to the palette,
dab flat, then spread it with a roller &
apply to the face of the block: press this to
paper, remove & reveal:
Ah.

Given to spasms of what must be mistake-laden
life pursuits, beautiful nooks & crannies
step by step in the tableau,
until the portcullis comes down
& the gel sticks:
Here—I—Am.
Ha.

The 'steady voice of realism',
the crystal pyramids of illusion,
the gaps between ethics & success,
perks optional.
What are the primal building blocks
& how do they fit together?
Bang.

Money-worries were his torment all his
adult life, a man-of-action over
grant application forms whose deadlines
made the sound of glass panels sliding
shut. Fub. Dark can chill you in yr path but
hope deals a welcome & a stark laugh.
Nurse what little light there is.
And nail the difference between
greed & being adventurous.

Squeeze some ink on to the palette,
dab flat, then spread it with a roller &
apply to the face of the block.

Thread-Bridge
[for clarinet]

Green part of a leaf
silver underpart

[sun pierce cloud]

birdcall among
trees then

[you]

a quiet comes down to which degree
of cloud-silence you find possible to

[sun through]

pool into one line as a finished mind
][that basket on the table will you][

[sun through]

battered notes
connected dots second hearings

scrapings over clumsy turns flu-
id mis-

[ ]

matchings cloud-words to
line up to surface abs-

[through]

orbing light quietly into its
place—dip brush-

tip to ink-pool glisten—cloud-cloud-cloud-cloud-
cloud—: begin.

It's Saturday again & you
sit down early to get some
work done in the tradition
of the First Strong Coffee &
the Niggling Idea, the Private
Space & the Public Domain.
Know what I mean? Planted.
Decide. This Old Tin-Opener
& the Closed Door. Hot Mug
of Tea in the Modern Imagination.
Art Made in a Shed—move a
plank, step, hammer it, step,
step back, to check, step-step—
in a Formal, Fragile Garden.
(Some neck).
      Water through a stone
mouth delivers a trickle of
tinkling jingles into a pool.
Laugh off the lichen gathering
on yr epitaph yellow & orange
blobs patches of vivid other-life
or scratch back well to fill yr
little dates in—*there's* deliberation!
Happy? That hill still. (Minimalism).
That cloud not. Take stock.
What date's today anyway?
A cat licks a forepaw in the light
then wipes its face, sits up alert
again then goes (maintaining) on.
                And yet…
Bubble-pops of pleasure
moving over the knuckles & thumbs,
the palm around the palm… a high
bright contrail heading south.

The prize is (this must be
what's-his-face by the way
on that copper horse of his
on its pedestal over there
in the cobbled square after
a spot of incinerating whole
villages locked into their
churches along with some
public torture of hand-picked
individuals to stay on top
wig & cheek streaked vivid
with pigeon shit) *now winter
nights enlarge the nombres
of their hours & clouds their
stormes discharge* the prize
is always visible. Which is
not quite the same thing as
tangibly in your pocket. Is it?

    Brush-tip to ink-pool:
        begin.

Jig: Blizzard

I read *Soap Tureen* for *Soup Tureen*.
I read *read* for *read*.

What's that meant to mean?

This to Say: Sonnet
[drums]

I have taken
the stones
that were on
the rice box

by the coloured
glass on the
windowledge
& put them in

the small ceramic
pot you made
what a decade
ago now with

its blue dots &
emphatic rim
fingertips a-tingle
in yr pocket

now that I look
noticing a note
under the magnet
on the fridge door

plumb the shadowy
dailiness sliced side-
ways into the career-
ing shiver of the actual

the that in which
probably forgive
thanks breakfast
sweet sweet sweet

& turned into English
what I thought I could
a common deviser of
slaunderous Pasquelles

nibb-
ling another
unbidden fruit
was

on the dice
box—what's that?—
a dish dashed
against

a plastic pane—
hidden in the
brittle Institute of
the World

I used to deem
the Paradigm
of the Obvious—
we did—yes—

    pop!

so cold
       so old
              so bold
& so sweet.

Good.

Rain Dance

Payment was taken in advance. A calm autumn morning,
a long correspondence, a yellow dust. A small stone.
A way through. One swan, two goldcrests. Ants scamper-
ing along threads of sugary meaning. In the dappled
court far away one lived a regulated life. It has been

asserted that love is/love is lacking in this work (from
these works). Chance. Dot. The children have been dressed
and (they have been) each in (her) turn taken home.
Beautifully surprising light-tracking, light-hungry, light-
enticing plants on the forest floor, tendril, panicle,

buttress. Travelling through their expertise, grim pingos,
treeless tundra (and that was the end of sweet Molly Mal-
who?) and getting (you did bring the sandwiches, yes?) really
a lot of (what?) nowhere fast (thanks), the God of Co-Co-Co-
Coherence in smithereens present and gaping at the terminus

wall changes everything. The man was taken back two days
after that. Dit-dot. What a moon! They did not talk (but)
only waited (there was no talking). They began (one began)
to speak of leading writers. Leading … *writers?* Dip. Dap.
    Tod. What on earth [my God] does that mean?

.

The first raindrop on the glass whose note is different to
the second and so the third—momentum, angle, mass—a
dance of—a fourth—and then a flicked spatter of several
more—a quiet dance for all that too, for you, here in the
dark, over yr head, comes together, speeds, spreads, then

slows—evenly—into a luminous quiet across each remembered
spot. It's not that Time(   )Flies, no, but that the past slip-
ping back & elasticated can-will *ping!* forward into a possible
future now/now any moment now any moment/moment (dash) duck!
now. It is important that the public should not be given a

false picture. Plumes of steam across dark industrial zones. Ear-tufts and ruffs, patterned wattles. Let's have a cup of tea (said Polymath to Polyglot). Let's certainly. Good, yes, thanks. A lot. High pressure, low cloud, where do we go from here? Close the windows,
  lock the house, it'll all be fine in the end, my dear…

        looked up dodging dogshit gladdened no
        matter sirens this must be
        nature

        though not my nature or yours for that/
        three to five pm/am
        could be

        twelve noon—who cares—look up—
        here we go under-
        ground

        touching the inner corners of the category
        then wince back
        shocked.

        learning takes a turn, butterflies pass.
        busy picturing the
        fabric of

        the sky—peaks—hollows—whirlpools—how
        wind in trees—& trees
        in air—

        of air at speed against birds that
        wheel
        &

        pivot over the bay—there's ground enough to
        go around/twice. &
        twice again.

a crease on a page. shadow. light.

When you were a little boy, then a little man, then
a big, bursting, raging young man, then calmer, calmer,
finally older and to the point and you could say, yes:
some small distinct shadows across an envelope on a desk
before posting, or, falling from the sky, one snowflake,
detached, its patterns of descent, its dance, with a
million others, and the wind—dashes, floats, twists,
slips, hovers—a little boy again. When payment is
taken in advance…

Setting
[for guitar]

Back that into a corner.
Park it over there. Let's
go to the park & take a
walk under its trees, leading
lines in steps together that
go back, back far (park that
car, let's go) branched &
growing still, moving, clicking
a little in this winter morning
breeze. Tap. Take care.

    Well, that's past.
    I taught that
    lesson & it's past.
    I drove past

    trees—not fast
    the traffic was
    terrible—& got
    there late at

    last. Of course.
    The special
    pleasure of step-
    ping over park-

    land peppered
    with last year's
    hardened beech
    mast or (you're

    an artist, yes?)
    the elasticity of
    time sluicing past
    its cast iron image

                of itself twisting
                in its flask to rip
                it & its brief
                occupants apart

                is worthy of note.
                Take heart. Don't
                fret. People are
                wonderful. But

                do they last? Let's
                take that walk

we talked about now (are you awake?)
along this black path, each footstep on
the map, block, each arm-swing, each
eye-face contact with what's outside,
connected in that bright dark pool (quick
strum) which I (we) think is inside you
for sure you call (block) what, yes, each
unplanned pebble-knock, each bird-dot
going by in opening twilight (it's dawn)
each whispered connection I know you
know about following & enwinding.
Good to be alive. A little longer. Along
the world-sheet. Out-&-about. To watch
our children. To imagine the next chord.

This must be an Affected Place. And *this*
must be another Affected Place; sharp
arrow arriving and pointing down. Where
the arrow lands, bury me. Placed. I remember
(I was very young indeed) perched on my
father's knee, he reading Robin Hood
to me in the garden by that purple shrub.
Life's arrow, life's Affected Places. Dodge
this arrow now—quick flick—divert from
that Place sharply, and remember: Design
for a Cloak, Underwater Pyramids, Light-
                Broadening,
                Illuminated
                Leaf.

Carpet of Memory

Including seeds…

including seeds gathered at the grass-tip, ready

including 33 East 50th St., New York City, 1948,
'both little fingers slightly deformed', in the biography,
echoing, through bureaucracy, detail, history, documents, death,
a small indentation, a change of mind.

Grind the berries, crush the tuber, move carefully
past each bright fibre as the dark ink sets, one
leaf opening, quick-step, grave. Twilight. Including,
including.

Understanding the Earth reads a title on a spine
on a shelf vertical to the ground it speaks of
in its place to my left, stock-still, spinning—oil—gold—
diamonds—while at the vellum-frame in a time-twist …

ivy clings & fidgets. Rain slams down.

…through which music must once have passed, your music,
moving out past each outpost, faintly able to continue in you,
in through other ghostly meshes too, windows, paper, marbling,
& out—cross-hatched—to where each leaf opens, each
connected stem, each registered ripple in the air against the wall,
your fingers, say, small, shadowy, where rain hits & branches
carry an after-rain slow-motion downpour of their own.

Including weeds

including the vigour of weeds

including the intricate bounty of weeds

& upstanding flowers & growth

& visiting insects   bees beetles flies caterpillars

Locket

Place yr cup

on the table

look up

what's that?

Uic aithan it is thought the Mayans responded
to the Conquistadors' *What is the name of your
land?* One foot, two. *What? We don't understand you.*

Hence Yucatán.

Let's live there then for a bit.

I am.

Poetry

The oldest seed ever known to germinate
was a 2,000-year-old date-palm seed
retrieved from archaeological excavations
of King Herod's palace. Seeds found during
the excavations lay in a drawer for 30 years
or more until someone thought they might try
to germinate them: one did.

```
The oldest seed ever known to germinate
was a 2,000 year old date- alm seed
        ved   om archaeolog    tions
of K         lace.        nd d
t          ay    a   wer         0




                              pa m


              x

t



                                        id




       il


rmin


                                              .
```

Mazurka

Then a flattened
out folded up
square

of paper—oh it's wet—let's see
… & blank?
dis-

appearing in a single
crisp collapse & a
Last Will &

Testament that would have been—
could have been—so kind
to you

shrivels into
an ugly
wizen.

Dots of silver glisten where a
snail's moved across
the grain

in turn shivered
under chainsaw
ridges

& here's where
the ivy's
cut.

But speaking of midwifery
who invented the
sporran,

the drum machine, the meticulously
embroidered pink-white
tight-fitting

toilet roll cover
perfect
for

yr B&B in synthetic cotton?
Such a talented nation.
                    Stem-thread.
                                Flower-shock.

            Birdsong
     under
a tree.

How many pebbles how much symmetry?
A frame a gasp a knock
a shadow.

Shutters open apart across a pool, a plate
of light thicken-
ing

fixed. So. The river the city a curve on a
map in
yr

pocket—move & you blur. Move yr
love in time
's little

gullet &—moved—stop. Move & you
pause at the top of
light's

whip-tip, ready. Move & you've been there.
Stop. Move. Stop.
Making

sense room frames fun games &—money. Is
that funny? Don't
smile.

    Click.

An interstitial blip-dance full of
I mean peppered
with I mean

shot through with glinting
air bubbles that pop
in rhythm

to the mystery. Indeed.
Pain. Thou hast
hands.

A lorry slowly moving
through the
estate

& somebody runs a tap
in the flat
next-door...

A paradigm's a
paradox
with

holes in it setting the
sea-view
free—

(tick) wipe lenses gently
taking sense
back

through them from
the other
side—

one foot, two. Know
what I mean? Sure
do
  (large, thin, medial, blade-like lip).

Odd patterns on woodchip wallpaper
oversee the little
cubicles

where Guardians of the Peace
accommodate
the poor

& rents accumulate
tax-free.

In
  this
    painful
       impermanent
           world.
What is fit & not. What is fit.

Yes, in every
interlude but
look—

I don't know: where there's
puke there's
food.

                              Then slap that Funk
                              & Wagnall &
                              let's go.

Pavane

What is the sound a spider makes moving over a leaf?

That sound.

Glazed cherry. It glistens. Is that a window bend-reflected in miniature on its skin? Look—it's for sale. Forever. *Poem*: the nature of the nature of the surface of reality has begun to laugh at me (again).

But can't you see the crud for the fees?

Interwoven bird-tracks on the sand.

That sound.

Yr hand. Thigh.

Duck of urgency paddles off. Across everything you ever imagined you might write.

'Yr mirror is ready, Sir.'

Crackling chitin palping a chrysalis, ridged fabric on a table.

The crow of intent. I dodge, you dodge, you look, I do, each missing the other, or I you—bloody parallax!—crumple up yr mind-screen, just go *see*.

Right.

Right.

Nurse!

Interconnected sound-hoops—fluid sentences—simplicities—hope-scraps—

in your wire shopping basket
in the queue.
Here I am.
How are you?

> *one torn envelope (one torn envelope)*
> *one torn envelope its shadows crevices*
> *planes jaggeds pleats colours whose white*
> *whose arena quietly assembling leaning on*
> *other papers whose pallor this envelope*
> *its wide v-fold its calm line its corners*
> *the quake of the broken points at its lip*
> *what it carried (across distance) (one)*
> *through storm sky cloud (one) day/night flicker*
> *(one) one torn envelope one torn envelope*

Simply imply.
Thanks. Press through check-out—
pass out—move on.
Are you happy?
Red wolves, jingle of change.
I'm impressed, are you?

Song Beginning 'When'

When the church bell rings hold on
a sec I mean when a recording of a
church bell is activated by a timer
from plastic speakers set into the
stone steeple of the local church
commemorating an angel visiting
a virgin with the news she is pregnant
the bell-beats warp in the strong wind
& driving rain of a December mid-day
in the half-dark that she is pregnant
miraculously & bearing a god. It was
a long, long time ago. And house &
car alarms come on in the wind. And the
strong smell of an idea slaps past & all's
well up there it seems, it seems in the
joined-up world, but here, here, buried
under History, you catch yr breath. And
mark this dark park in the Atlantic.
Maybe a year since suddenly I began
sipping hot tea in a cold shed—teaching
the future to my students—long gone—
to Sweden, to Norway, to China, Japan—
now—premeditated, unpremeditated,
time-tabled, calendrical, predicted
(given evidence) & so on—in the car
as we sped through time & the rhymes
rippled—place yr foot there, then place
it there, turn, turn round—rippled a
little in song through time past tree
by tree by two or three possibilities that
hit & melt on the windscreen & are gone.
Remember? The slightly, almost hollow
sound a fresh apple makes when you rub it.
        When. On earth.
        The past.
        Your mother might know.

Echo

In Gilbert White's
letter of February
12th 1778 he
discusses at length
the echo effect
of a particular
point on a path
in his parish.
Reading this
this morning I
remember now
that just yesterday
I happened
to take
my copy of
*The Autumn-Born
in Autumn*
up from my desk
& as chance would
have it, it fell
open at a poem
called *Echo*.
Why not. Next.
Turning the
page now
I find it's
dated 2nd June 1778
& turn white.
Tick. It's
the 2nd of June
as I write.
Why not ask
Isobel Mawne
if she could come
as a supply teacher
to the infants' room
to replace Miss Briggs?

X. P. K.
The second
2nd June
second by second.
Stopped.
Watched. To the
letter. Must.

When exactly
are you born
when exactly
do you fade away
acting now in fact
in a gliding dhow
in sunlight
in the channel
in Gibraltar
exactly yes
now when
left-hand
margins seem
to make a
blade to
let other bits
& bobs barge in
then cut—
              cut—
                          cut—
& why not
if disaster
or dishonour strike
or exultant glory
end yr story
with a shiny ribbon
tight about its
awkward bulk amen
& the tide turn
& yr language die
yr little house

burn down—
nothing fixed
nothing broken
nothing known—
knowing no branch
in any tree anymore
anywhere anyway—
what then?
      O.

Better.

Coda

Village & Interior
[with glockenspiel]

Birds in the street
below, mingle of
voices that come
& go on what flows
in as the faintest ghost
of a spirit-breeze, a
butterfly closing its
wings in the world some-
where without a sound.
Bing. Back. Bong goes
the little metal bell
over the village in
the heat, yellow &
ochre tiles tilt & slant
over hidden laneways
in the shade, a black
cat disappears, a moth
lands & shivers from
elsewhere out of the blue,
blinds come down, several
strangely heavy crumbs
of rock that are bright red
now in this light seem
poised to drop through a
crack in the church-
tower on the hill that
hasn't widened in a very
long time they say
around here,
                yet.

      What?

Stand back so that you can
look at what you think you
might have made, before it

    falls apart, before it becomes
    a part of background noise,
      a ripple within a ripple
        within a chaos …
          Poise.
      Tap on the drum.

    Branches bend to my will,
    the speckled ratbird calls
    through cold air, kernels
    moisten in their fruit, fat.
        Tap:

        an apple
        by a pond
        where a
        pebble drops.

          Again.
          Listen.

          Again.

I have eaten
the plums
that were in
the icebox

and which
you were probably
saving
for breakfast

Forgive me
they were
delicious

so cold
  tart
    dark.

Jig

This is a day.
This is a moment
in a day. This
is the point of

intersection of
a moment in a day.
This is its noise.
This is a series

of flashes. This
is a further series
bled into crevices
& burnt back on

to each other—like
that. Crackling
densities: one view-
point wedged into

another & stuck on
a plinth. Hang on a sec:
I'll get it. Threads
meshed & taut &

the fabric bound
down tight &
wet: today's date
& place—tomorrow's.

The next. Click past.
Listen. Listen.
Listen to roots grow
into crevices of

what must be let's see
yr name &—ah yours—
& yours—a tin hat &
a hard neck—

all those small vowels
nestling among tough
consonants

chipped & gnarled
those pools of isolation
among rock that swirl &
dip along

the world-line
then flow on
to strange locations
in no time at all.

This is an ikon.
This is the way that
it shimmers. This
is its surface.

This is that surface
split open where
each split blisters
& each blister figures

a little as it were
canyon seen from above—
far—human limitation
(limitation limitation)

gimme the Huuuman
Limit-at-tation Blues—
delve down then into
its jagged cracks—

shadows—spikes—
splinters—delight—
process. These are
the bits that stick.

Orbit

When the astronauts ejected their

urine into space it froze of course

instantly but

what

they hadn't quite expected

was how its delicate crystalline

beauty against the vast black stood fixed

(Dapple

Notes

Some snippets of the Irish language appear in the text.

p.23: *'S an t-airgead?*: 'And the money?'

> *I dteanga an ghasúir—rince.*
> 'In the boy's language—dance.'

p.40: *Baint an Fhéir*, hay-making. A popular *céilí* dance.

p.48: *Do Bhíos Lá i bPortláirge*: 'One day I was in Waterford', a traditional song.

p.49: *glé-* a prefix meaning: 'bright, pure, glistening'

p.87:
> *cride é*
> *daire cnó*
> *ócán é*
> *pócán dó*

> he is my heart
> fruit of the oak [acorn]
> he's a young man
> a kiss for him

…

p.44: Lesotho, pronounced 'Lesutu'

p.47: ELIGP: 'Eternal Learning Institute of the Gaelic Phantasm'

p.61: *Rain [signed piece]*: 'Signature' folded into phrases like 'forest gully', 'or is dully…'; the stanza count, that of the author's age at time of composition.

p.68: *A Stupendous Idea*: The next sentence reads: 'Why not ask Isobel Mawne if she could come as a supply teacher to the infants' room to replace Miss Briggs?' From the *Thrush Green* series by Miss Read.

Frontispiece based on glyphs from the rongorongo tablets, undeciphered.

Backing Vocals

The kids leave for
school now in a haze of
colour at the door—
it must be love—love—

love—caught in the quick
of living & breathing I
think I'll leave this note
for them here too—

reverof DNA
        yawa DNA

I've left the wooden
tray on the table
set for when you
waken

I've taken
the tom-toms
that were in
their bright box

by the speakers that
keep crackling,
the old school of
hard knocks,

losers weepers, you
know the story, the
linguistic theatre of
delight, snap, click

those fingers, look
round & bow, dogs
barking at defunct
neighbours funct

pissed in the middle
of the night bang—
clatter—keys tinkling—
pocket-fumbling

&—hey—life is sweet—
tip-top—take note—rock
bottom too—a busy man
do-wap that's me—

a graduate cum laude
tapping out messages
to the enemy, making
friends.

That sit on committees
that give me prizes
& praise me a little
too loudly now that

I think of it—is that a
fox in the street?—there's
the phone—I'll get it—
a door slams shut—then …

back to sleep. Good.
Tap. Then I woke up.

As the sickly sweet-sticky pustules on the
rind of the fat fruit flatten of a sudden
on the path on impact with a red slap in front
of you you think *phew!* I'm not famous, I
don't live here under the Fame Tree, just
passing through…

reverof DNA
    yas-yas ot   esimorp ot
        yas-evig ot   yned ot
    yas-ekat ot yawa DNA
                    nogaw yddap
spmuht   spals   neercsdniw   tips

Maurice Scully was born in Dublin on 2nd June 1952. He has published close on a dozen books over the last 35 years.

A Sprinkling of Friends from Caxley

It was
the last day of the holiday
& it ended very
pleasantly

for me
with a little party
at Holly
Lodge

where
Henry Mawne's nephew David,
(sister of Horace Umbleditch)
now lived.

The older Mawnes were there
& also David's boy
Simon
as well as

the vicar
& his wife
&
    a

sprinkling
       of
            friends
                    from
                          Caxley.

Exactly. I'd been reading Gilbert White's letter
of Feb 12th 1778 where he discusses at length the
echo effect of a particular point on a path in his
parish when I took up my copy of *The Autumn-Born
in Autumn*, & as chance would have it, it fell open
at a poem called *Echo*. Now. I'm writing this in
January with snow on the hills giving back the hills
to a white-still sky. So little can tilt the lens when
the split sack spills open to the listening eye as you
imagine it beginning to blink between a floating 'now'
& some stopped 'past' in a cracked forgotten take
on human history. Whatever. *Forever* is printed on the
doormat to these premises. But wait: think straight—
is that you now in fact in a gliding dhow in sunlight
in the Straits of Gibraltar or just past Zanzibar
all lined up I reckon though not yet ready to know
how far exactly a life across the ocean wave could go
when or how fast or however otherwise by water could it
be so made for a s/lavish little copycat like you…

                well done   tact

                              pen   star

                    silt

                        salty

                                centre

                                              flint
                    skint

                          format

                                    slit   bitten

                    done

                                      bell

                                                smack

www.ingramcontent.com/pod-product-compliance
Lightning Source LLC
Chambersburg PA
CBHW031151160426
43193CB00008B/336